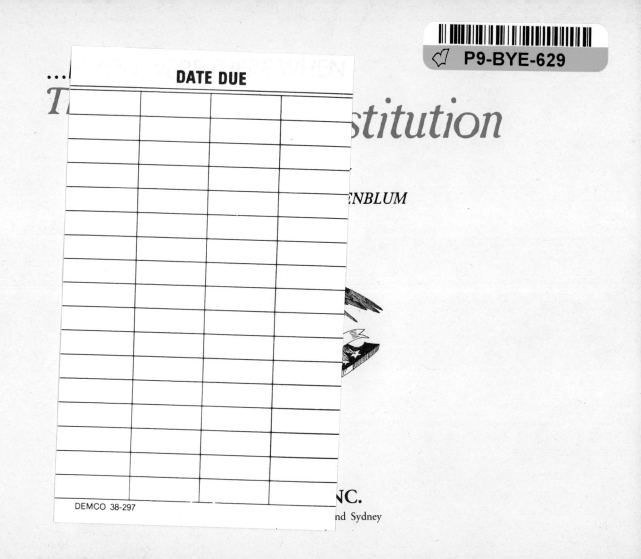

...WERE YOU THERE WHEN

T...stitution

...ENBLUM

...NC.

...nd Sydney

ISBN 0-590-40519-5

Copyright © 1987 by Elizabeth Levy.
Illustrations copyright ©1987 by Scholastic Books, Inc.
All rights reserved. Published by Scholastic Inc.
Art direction by Diana Hrisinko.
Text design by Emmeline Hsi.

12 11 10 9 8 7 6 5 4 3   7 8 9/8 0 1 2/9

Printed in the U.S.A.   08
First Scholastic printing, August 1987

To Bill Harris and KidsPac who proved,
as our founding fathers knew, that good politics,
good eating, good drinking, and fun go together.

Many thanks to Professors Thomas Cronin
and Marvin Gettleman, who gave generously
of their time in reading the manuscript.

Special thanks to Professor Forrest
McDonald, who taught me more about
writing than even he knew.

Special thanks also to writer Robie Harris,
who also gave generously of her time
in reading drafts of this manuscript, and who
lived through the summer of its writing.
The writing of the Constitution may have
only taken three months, but the writing of
this book took considerably longer.

Special thanks to Professor George Vickers,
who also lived through my Constitutional
summer of 1986.

E.L.

CONTENTS

What is the Constitution?

The Constitution of the United States is the basic law of our nation — like the rules for a game, only these rules are for the government, and all citizens must play.

The Constitution sets up the rules for how laws are made, and who will make the laws. Who will decide if we go to war? Who will have power? You? Me? You can find those answers in the Constitution.

The Constitution of the United States was written in 1787. It has lasted two hundred years, longer than any other written constitution. The men who wrote it wanted their new nation to last. They knew how hard it was to create a government that could change with the times. After all, they had just fought and won a war against a government that had refused to change. That war was the American Revolution.

American rebels in New York City tore down a metal statue of King George. The statue was melted and made into bullets for fighting the Revolution.

Why did we go to war?

For over one hundred years, we were colonies that belonged to England and ruled by the King. In 1763, King George III began to demand more taxes from the American colonies. People didn't like having to pay a tax on every little thing — on paper, glass, and tea. But they had no one to speak for them in England. "No taxation without representation!" they cried.

After a while, many Americans wanted to rebel, to break away from England, and become independent.

What was the Declaration of Independence?

On July 4, 1776, the Declaration of Independence officially declared the American colonies free and independent. It has become one of the most famous documents in the world. It declares that all men are created equal. It said that the thirteen colonies were now thirteen free states — free from the King and England. But notice, it didn't say that the thirteen states were united. The rebels didn't know if they could win their revolution. One-third of the people in the colonies stayed loyal to the King.

One of the signers of the Declaration of Independence was Benjamin Franklin. He begged the thirteen new states to work together. "We must all hang together, or assuredly, we shall all hang separately," he said.

What did the King of England think of the Declaration of Independence?

Ben Franklin was right. King George wanted to hang all the rebels. The King sent more than one hundred ships full of soldiers to fight the American rebels. General George Washington led the Revolution against England.

During the long revolutionary war, General Washington gathered around him young men from all over the thirteen states. These young men thought of themselves as fighting for a nation, not for their own state back home. Washington treated them like the sons he never had.

Six years after the Revolution, in 1787, several of these young men would go to Philadelphia with George Washington to help write the Constitution.

What rules did the thirteen states have before the Constitution?

The thirteen states knew they couldn't fight a revolution without helping each other. Right in the middle of the Revolution, they wrote a set of rules for themselves. They called this agreement the Articles of Confederation. Under the Articles of Confederation, the thirteen states elected a Congress, a group of people to make laws. In this Congress each state had one vote, no matter how many people lived in that state. The Articles could not be changed unless every state agreed.

How well did Congress work under the Articles of Confederation?

Not very well at all. The rebel government needed money to fight the war, but there was no way to make the states pay up. If the fighting was in New York, the states far away would not send money. General Washington had to go to Congress again and again to beg for bullets, food, and clothes for his rebel soldiers.

James Madison from Virginia was a young rebel congressman. He wanted to help Washington and his soldiers. He decided that the Articles of Confederation did not work, because Congress could not make the states tax people to pay for the war.

J. MADISON

A. HAMILTON

Alexander Hamilton was a young aide de camp to General Washington. In 1780, while the Revolution was still going on, he wrote, "There is only one remedy — to call a convention of all the states, and the sooner the better." Alexander Hamilton and James Madison were two of the leaders of the fight to get a new Constitution.

Why didn't the thirteen states unite into a real nation during the Revolution?

The states were fighting a war to make sure they weren't ruled and taxed by a government far away. The rebels wanted to control their own lives.

During the Revolution most states wrote their own constitutions. Each state elected its own leaders. They were proud to be free of kings.

One reason nobody thought the thirteen states could be one nation was that we were so big: ten times bigger than most other countries, twelve hundred miles long from north to south. It took weeks for people to get news from one state to another.

This map shows the 13 original states.

*What is now the state of Maine was owned by Massachusetts.

**What is now the state of Vermont was claimed by New Hampshire and New York.

If you lived in Boston, you probably thought of your nation as the state of Massachusetts. Your money wasn't good in Rhode Island. When William Houston of Georgia went to New York, he wrote that he was leaving "his country to go to a strange land amongst strangers."

What happened after we won the Revolutionary War?

It was a time of great experiments in government. The newly free states enjoyed making their own rules. But they had many problems, especially with foreign countries.

England had lost the war, but she refused to leave the forts in the West, even though the peace treaty said she must. "Make me," said England.

We had no way of making anyone do anything. The minute the Revolution was over, the men in the army went home. Nobody had paid their wages for months. Nobody wanted to pay taxes. There was no way to make England give up the forts.

That wasn't all.

•Pirates at sea caught American citizens and put them into slavery.

•The thirteen states could not agree on how to deal with the Indian tribes nor what to do with the western territories.

•Spain owned all the land west of the Mississippi and wouldn't allow any Americans to use the Mississippi River south of Natchez.

Until the thirteen states could find a way to speak with one voice, no foreign country would have to listen.

And *that* wasn't all.

Most people in the new states were farmers. After the war, prices went up. Many farmers owed a lot of money.

In those times if you couldn't pay your debts, you could go to jail. Soon many farmers found themselves in jail.

In 1786 in Massachusetts, Daniel Shays, a hero of the Revolution, led a group of farmers in a revolt against the state of Massachusetts. They wanted to keep their farms and get help for their debts.

Shays' Rebellion didn't get very far. Shays and his men were defeated. Four people were killed, and most of the rebel farmers fled into the woods. But news of Shays' Rebellion scared people. They were afraid

the revolt of the farmers would spread. The new national government had not been able to help Massachusetts.

General Washington was alarmed. "I am mortified beyond expression," he said, "when I view the clouds that have spread over the brightest morn that ever dawned in any country. What a triumph for our enemies."

But Thomas Jefferson, another leader of the American Revolution, was not worried. "I like a little rebellion now and then," he wrote. "The spirit of resistance to government is so valuable on occasion that I wish it to be always kept alive."

Did Shays' Rebellion lead to the writing of the Constitution?

Historians have argued for years about exactly how and why we came to write the Constitution. Were the writers scared that the Revolution had brought too much liberty? Or did they want to make sure that their Revolution lasted?

Certainly Shays' Rebellion shook up many people. But there were many other reasons why people wanted a new constitution. George Washington and other leaders of the Revolution wanted to see a stronger united nation. They wanted this nation to have only one money system. They wanted a nation that could trade with other governments.

They felt we needed to be one nation to make treaties with Europe. We needed an

army and navy if we had to go to war again. They were looking for any excuse to try to bring the states together to write a new constitution.

How did the thirteen states finally agree to meet in Philadelphia?

James Madison had the bright idea to use a quarrel between two states as an excuse to bring all the states together. Virginia and Maryland started fighting over whose ships could go up and down the Potomac, the river that was the boundary of both states. Madison called for a convention at Annapolis, Maryland, in September 1786, to discuss the problem of trade between all the states.

Only five out of the thirteen states sent

delegates. (A delegate is someone chosen to speak and act for a group.) With so few delegates, very little could be done.

But Alexander Hamilton came to Annapolis from New York. He and James Madison decided not to give up. They called for another conference to be held in Philadelphia on the second Monday of May, 1787. It was at this convention in Philadelphia that our Constitution was written.

Of course, at that time, no one called it the Constitutional Covention. They didn't know they were going to write a constitution. They called it the "Grand Convention" or the "Federal Convention."

What happened when the Convention opened?

Almost nothing. It had been the rainiest spring in history. All the roads were mud. Hardly anyone showed up on time. On opening day only a few Virginians and the men who lived in Philadelphia were there. Poor James Madison, who had come eleven days early, was practically alone. For a while it looked as though there would never be a convention.

George Washington arrived on Sunday, May 13, 1787, the day before the Convention was to begin. The sun came out for the first time in weeks. Washington was met by a number of his old troops, all in uniform and shiny black boots. The people stood on the cobblestone streets and cheered and cheered.

As soon as Washington arrived, he called on the only other man in America as famous as he, Dr. Benjamin Franklin.

We do not know what Washington and Franklin talked about. They might have met under the mulberry tree in Franklin's garden, a favorite place for him to sit. We do know that Franklin laid in a good bottle of port for them to drink.

Where did the delegates stay?

Many delegates stayed at the Indian Queen, an inn very close to the State House where they would be meeting. A young black servant with powdered hair and a red cape met them at the door. So many delegates stayed at the Indian Queen that the landlord set aside a special dining room for them.

George Washington stayed at the home of his good friend Robert Morris, who was also a delegate to the Convention. Morris had helped get the money to fight the Revolution. Morris would end up in jail for his debts, but in 1787, he was one of the richest men in Philadelphia.

What did they do while they waited for enough people to show up?

The early arrivals had to wait until delegates from at least seven states arrived before the Convention could begin. They went to parties and taverns. Philadelphia was the largest city in America, and there was much to see and do. But mostly the early arrivals talked and argued about what to do about writing a constitution.

James Madison had a plan. He had spent a whole year reading everything he could on government. For all his quiet and bookish ways, Madison was a very smart politician. He knew that if he could get his plan talked about first, other people might never get a chance to bring up their own plans.

Madison's plan would come to be called the Virginia Plan. The Virginia Plan did away with the "one state — one vote" rule in the old Articles of Confederation. Under the Virginia Plan the new Congress would be based on how many people lived in each state. If one state had more people than another, it would have more power.

Madison's plan gave the national government real power over the states. It would be able to make war, control trade and money.

When the Convention finally opened, where did the delegates meet?

They met at the Pennsylvania State House or, as people were already beginning to call it, Independence Hall. It was here that

Thomas Jefferson had first read his Declaration of Independence to many of the same men who were now gathering to write the Constitution.

Behind the building was a garden, or mall, as it was called. The trees on the mall were small then, and they didn't give much shade in the hot sun of the summer.

Across the street was the city jail, a stone prison, four stories high. Many of the people were in there because they could not pay their debts. As the delegates walked to work, the inmates of the jail would stick out their hats on long poles and beg for money.

You can still visit Independence Hall today, and it looks very much the same. It is a graceful red brick building with tall windows.

The Convention was mostly held in the East Room, a comfortable room about forty feet by forty feet, probably more than twice the size of your classroom, but smaller than your gym. The delegates sat at round tables covered with green cloths, about three or four to a table.

When you visit Independence Hall, you immediately feel that this is a good room for a debate — not too fancy, yet filled with light from the great tall windows on each side.

Finally on Friday, May 25, 1787, there were enough delegates to begin.

What were the delegates like?

They were all white men, and they were far richer than the average person who lived at that time. Tiny Rhode Island refused to send anybody to the Convention. The other twelve states elected seventy-four delegates. But only fifty-five delegates showed up. On most days there were only thirty or forty delegates working.

The youngest delegate was Jonathan Dayton of New Jersey, who was twenty-seven. The oldest delegate was Ben Franklin, who was eighty-one. Most of the leaders were in their early thirties. Thirty of the delegates had served in the army during the revolutionary war.

Half of them were lawyers. All of them were well known in their states.

But there is no way that numbers can tell you about them. Let's look more closely at a few of them.

JONATHAN DAYTON

What was Ben Franklin like?

Benjamin Franklin couldn't resist trying out new ideas. Many of his new ideas were about science. He invented the lightning rod, bifocals, and the Franklin stove.

He also thought of new political ideas. He helped write the Declaration of Independence. In 1783, he helped write the peace treaty with England.

By 1787, he was an old man, in his eighties. He was so sick that he didn't think he could do much at the Convention, but he knew he was needed. He had to be carried to the Convention in a chair on four long poles carried by four convicts who he hired from the jail for the day. It was the first sedan chair ever seen in this country.

What was George Washington like?

George Washington was the most famous delegate at the Convention. After the Revolution, many people thought General Washington would make himself king. People loved and respected him. He was really our first national hero.

He was a proud man, and prickly. He had a quick temper and could burst into a rage and bellow like a bull. He was fearless.

He was fifty-five at the time of the Convention, but he had more energy than men half his age. He loved to ride his horses at top speed. He could dance for three hours at a time.

He wore false teeth, made of ivory, not wood, and they didn't fit very well. His false teeth made it hard for him to talk, so

sometimes he didn't like to speak in public. But he loved to be with people, and he loved to listen. He would go to the tavern and share in the gossip. He had so much company that he once said that he and his wife hadn't dined alone for twenty years.

Who was Alexander Hamilton, and what was he like?

Alexander Hamilton was a delegate from New York State. He was born in the West Indies. He was probably one of the smartest young men at the Convention. Some people at the Convention said he was too smart for his own good. He would go on to become our first secretary of the treasury.

Hamilton was small and good-looking. Men at that time wore tight pants called breeches that ended at the knee. They also wore stockings, sometimes of silk. Sometimes men with skinny calves put bags of sand under their stockings to look like muscles. Occassionally, the sandbags would leak over the floor and the ladies would giggle, but Hamilton never had need of sandbags in his stockings. People said he had a "graceful turn of the leg."

Who was Gouverneur Morris?

Gouverneur Morris was a delegate from Pennsylvania. He was another of the young men who had helped George Washington in the Revolution. Gouverneur Morris was a wealthy young man. He lost a leg in an accident, but he still managed to dance on his wooden leg.

Gouverneur Morris was always up for a joke. One night he boasted that he wasn't afraid of the proud George Washington. He made a bet to slap George Washington on the back.

The next day, he thought better of it. He didn't actually slap Washington on the back, he just put his hand on Washington's arm.

"The great man turned and looked at me, and I wished the earth had yawned and swallowed me up," wrote Morris afterward.

What was James Madison like?

James Madison is often called the father of the Constitution. He was short—five feet six. "No bigger than half a piece of soap," said a man who knew him. He had pale blue eyes and brown hair.

He never had to work for a living. His father had built up an estate of thousands of acres with many slaves in Virginia.

Most wealthy young men in the South were expected to ride, hunt, and drink. But Madison loved to read. He was shy.

He thought of himself as sickly, but as the historians Christopher and James Collier said, "In an age when few diseases could be cured, he was rarely sick. He went from one high-pressure job to another — member of Virginia government, congressman, secretary of state, President. He was a politician until his death at eighty-five."

Who were William Paterson, Roger Sherman, and Luther Martin?

William Paterson was from New Jersey. He was a lawyer and a very hard worker. He would soon become a Supreme Court justice.

Roger Sherman was from Connecticut. He was a farmer and a shoemaker, and he was one of the few "self-made" men at the Convention. He was round, with a rather large head. "He's the oddest-shaped character I ever remember to have met with," said a fellow delegate. Sherman was a clever debater.

WILLIAM PATTERSON

ROGER SHERMAN

LUTHER MARTIN

Luther Martin was from Maryland. He was one of the strangest men at the Convention. His family was poor. He was a brilliant lawyer, but he sometimes drank too much. It is said he once bumped into a cow and said "Excuse me." And sometimes he would just talk on and on.

Chances are you haven't heard of these men. All three fought against Madison's plan — and lost. "History is written by the winners," say some historians.

What were the two sides at the Convention?

Madison, Franklin, Washington, Hamilton, Gouverneur Morris, and Robert Morris were all "nationalists." They wanted to see a great united nation come out of the Convention.

Paterson, Sherman, Martin, and others worried that men like Alexander Hamilton and Gouverneur Morris did not care enough about liberty. They thought a huge united nation would take away some of the freedoms they had won during the Revolution. These people wanted to make sure that the states kept their rights. Some call these men the "states rights" people.

41

Both sides had studied history. They knew they had made history by fighting and winning a revolution. They studied England, and they admired the way England had a parliament. They studied ancient history. Each side wanted to create a republic — a government without a king — that would be strong yet free. They argued about how to do this.

Who did both sides admire?

George Washington, of course. Many of the people had come to Philadelphia because they knew General George Washington would be there. The delegates had to elect a chairman. Everyone knew it would be Washington. Ben Franklin wanted to nominate

Washington, but it was raining (again!), and Franklin was too sick to leave his house that day.

Every single delegate voted for George Washington as chairman.

Washington walked up to a low platform where he sat facing the other delegates. He sat on a graceful open-back chair, not at all like a throne, but on its back was a carved and gilded sun, cut off at the horizon. Was it a rising or setting sun? Nobody could tell.

After Washington took his seat, James Madison did something for which all historians have been grateful.

"I chose a seat in front," he wrote, so that he could hear and write down all that happened and was said. "I was not absent a single day," said Madison. "Nor more than a fraction of an hour in any day."

Sometimes the speeches would go on for hours, but at the end of each day, Madison went back to the Indian Inn and wrote out his daily notes, sometimes more than twenty pages, all written neatly with a quill pen.

Madison would not allow his notes to be published until the last delegate died. Guess who it was. It turned out to be James Madison himself, who died in 1836.

What two rules helped make the Convention a success?

First, the delegates decided to keep everything they said secret. This meant that people could say things that they might not want to be reported back home.

The delegates were serious about keeping things secret. They put guards at the windows. They even nailed the windows shut. It would turn out to be the hottest summer in years. This was before air conditioning or even electric fans. You can imagine how hot it got.

Second, they allowed the delegates to change their minds. Even if a vote had been taken on an issue, someone could bring it up again. Whenever the delegates argued so much that they were afraid they'd split up, they could take a vote, then go on to something else, knowing that they could come back to the problem.

If you and your classmates were making up a new game, and you got into a huge argument about the rules, how would you keep one group from walking out?

You'd need to find rules, as the delegates did, that would keep people talking until a compromise could be found. We will find out about all sorts of compromises in our Constitution.

What is a compromise?

A compromise settles an argument because each side gives up some of its demands. Suppose every week you want to watch one TV show, and your sister wants to watch another. You could have a fight every week, or you could watch your show one week and her show the next. Sometimes it's hard to compromise.

The Large State Plan

What was the first big argument?

James Madison's plan was presented first, and the little states hated it.

The Virginia Plan did away with the "one state-one vote" rule. The Virginia Plan called for two branches — or "houses" — of Congress. The first house would be based on the number of people in each state. The members of that house would elect members of the other, smaller house.

The small states were shocked. They weren't dumb. They saw that the big states would have more power in each house of the new Congress. They didn't want that.

For a while it looked like the Convention might split up. Gunning Bedford, from Delaware, said, "I do not, gentlemen, trust you. Will you crush the small states?"

Then the small states presented their own plan.

47

What was the small states' plan?

William Paterson of New Jersey put out his own plan that called for a Congress with just one house that would be based on the old system where each state would be equal. For nearly seven weeks as the weather got hotter and hotter, and the windows remained nailed shut, the delegates fought, sometimes voting this way, sometimes voting the other.

Luther Martin got up to speak for the New Jersey Plan. He talked on and on, driving the delegates crazy. "It might have gone on for two months had not the Convention showed its boredom," wrote one of the delegates.

Finally, the delegates decided to give the whole problem to a committee to try to come up with a compromise.

Article I establishes the two houses of Congress and their powers.

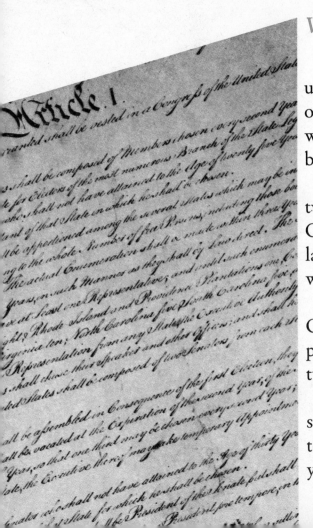

What was the "Great Compromise"?

We have lived for two hundred years under the compromise the delegates worked out. It seems natural to us. Can you guess what it is? Roger Sherman suggested it weeks before it was accepted on July 16.

It seemed simple. Congress would have two houses just like James Madison wanted. Only one house would be based on population, and in the other house each state would be equal.

And that's how it has been ever since. Our House of Representatives is based on population, and members are elected every two years.

In our Senate, all states are equal. Every state has two votes. Tiny Delaware is equal to California. Senators are elected every six years.

49

Together the House of Representatives and the Senate make up Congress. It took the delegates nearly two months to hammer out this compromise, and when they did they faced another, even bigger problem.

What was the problem hidden in the "Great Compromise"?

The problem was how to count the slaves. There were six hundred thousand black Americans in the country (twenty percent of the population). Ninety percent of them were slaves in the South.

The writers of the Constitution had gotten themselves into a pickle with their "Great Compromise," and they didn't know what to do. Under the Compromise, the more

people a state had, the more representatives it would have, and the more power. The southern states wanted to count their slaves as people. Of course, the slaves could not vote, but women and children were counted as people, and they couldn't vote, either.

The northern states didn't want to count the slaves. They argued that if slaves could be bought and sold they were no different from horses or mules. Gouverneur Morris said slavery was "the curse of heaven. Are they men? Then make them citizens and let them vote."

Once again the delegates worked out a compromise. Slaves would be counted as three-fifths, in other words five slaves would count as three whites.

What other compromises did the North make with the South?

Although most people in the North were not ready to end slavery altogether, many, many people hated the slave trade.

Almost everyone had heard horror stories about the long voyage from West Africa. Men, women, and children were chained to their bunks, lying like logs so the ships could fit in as many as possible. Many slaves tried to kill themselves by jumping overboard.

The South was afraid that a new national government would write a law that would stop the slave trade.

During the summer of 1787, the men in Philadelphia were not the only ones struggling with the question of slavery.

There was still an old Congress under the

In 1787, many Americans were beginning to move to the wild country west of the Ohio River. The land was called the Northwest Territory. Congress passed a law saying there would be no slavery in this land.

Articles of Confederation, and this Congress was still meeting in New York City. Many people, like Madison, were going back and forth between New York and Philadelphia.

In the middle of the summer, the old Congress settled a long debate. Would the land in the West be settled by free men or by slaves? Congress passed the Northwest Ordinance, which said that all land North of the Ohio River would be "forever free." No slavery would be allowed there. Alexander Hamilton and James Madison came back down to Philadelphia and told the delegates what had happened in Congress.

Today, some historians think that a deal was made. The North had won in the Northwest. Now the South was going to get its way in the Constitution.

Is the word "slave" in the Constitution?

No. If you read the original Constitution you can see that they never use the word "slave" or "slavery."

Our Constitution is mostly written in clear and beautiful English. But when it came to slavery, the delegates used very confusing words. They didn't want to put the word "slave" into their Constitution.

The Constitution has lasted two hundred years, but it was almost destroyed during the Civil War over the issue of slavery. During the Civil War, Abraham Lincoln would say "the word 'slavery' was hid away in the Constitution just as an afflicted man hides away a cancer which he dares not cut out at once, lest he bleed to death."

Abraham Lincoln was President in 1865 when Congress amended the Constitution to make slavery illegal.

54

Did the delegates do nothing but fight?

No. In fact some historians think that they agreed more than they disagreed. Almost all the delegates had been rebels against the King of England. They believed that the King had too much power.

"If men were angels," said James Madison, "no government would be necessary. If angels were to govern men . . . no controls on government would be necessary."

Basically, the delegates agreed with Madison. They knew their greatest challenge was to set up a government with enough power to act, but they wanted to be sure that the government did not have too much power.

The delegates wanted their new government to have different branches that could check each other. They thought the best government had what they called "separation of powers" and "checks and balances." That meant that no one person, or one group could make laws for everyone else.

How did the delegates invent a President?

The men at Philadelphia knew first hand what it was like to be ruled by a king. They wanted to make sure that no one man would ever have as much power as a king.

But on the other hand, they had lived for twelve years under a system when there was

PRESIDENT

KING

no head of the government, and that hadn't worked very well.

At the Philadelphia Convention during the hot summer, they had invented a House of Representatives and a Senate to make up the laws. But what if the House and the Senate voted foolish laws? Who would stop them? Would we have to go through another revolution?

No, they wanted a government where there would be someone strong enough to "check" the House and Senate, but not so strong that he could make himself king. They wanted someone who could lead the country in times of emergency and deal with the heads of other nations. They decided to call this person "President."

What does the President do?

The President cannot make laws. Only Congress can make laws, but the President has to carry out the laws. And the President can suggest laws.

One of the most important things any government has to decide is when and if to go to war. The delegates believed this was too big a question for one person to decide. It seemed to them that kings were always going to war and sending people to their deaths.

The delegates made the President Commander in Chief of the Army, but the President can not declare war on another country. Only Congress can declare war.

Article II establishes the office of President and its powers.

Who would be President?

The truth was that everyone in the room knew exactly who would be the first President. They had been looking at him all summer. It was George Washington.

But they knew Washington wouldn't live forever. Remember, they were inventing a new office: President. Who should pick the President?

They went round and round on this question. First they voted that the President should be picked by the Senate, but then they didn't like that.

James Wilson from Philadelphia kept arguing that the President should be elected by the people as a whole. This was a lot for the delegates to swallow. It was rare for anyone in Georgia to know anyone in Massachusetts. How would anyone ever know who would be the best President?

In the end the delegates made up an "electoral college." Although the electoral college is a strange and complicated system, James Wilson was right. Almost from the beginning, the President came to be seen as not just from one state, but as someone who has to represent all the people.

Why is the President elected for four years?

Alexander Hamilton suggested that the President be elected for life. That idea sent some of the delegates screaming that he wanted to set up a king — just what they didn't want to happen.

Some delegates thought the President should be elected for seven years. Some said three. Finally the delegates compromised on four.

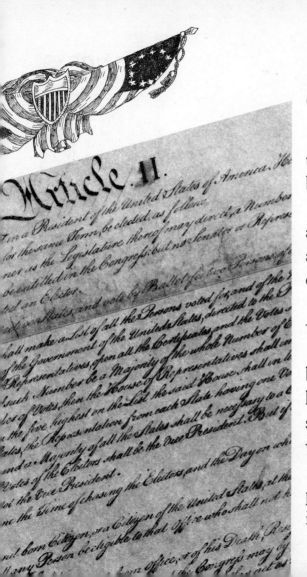

Who would make the laws? Congress or the President?

It takes both Congress and the President to make a law. There are a lot of checks and balances built into the system.

Suppose a member of Congress suggests a law making everyone eat peanut butter and mayonnaise sandwiches for lunch every day.

"That's crazy!" you might say. But how would you stop the law?

The delegates wanted to make sure that before any suggestion became a law it would have to go through many steps, and at each step it could be "checked" or stopped if it was a bad law.

An awful lot of people would have to like peanut butter and mayonnaise before having it for lunch became the law.

61

How are laws passed?

A law begins with a proposal called a *bill*. Most bills can start in either the House of Representatives or the Senate, but before a bill becomes a law, both branches of Congress must vote for it.

Then the President gets the bill. If he or she doesn't like it, the President can say no, or veto it. (*Veto* comes from the Latin word "forbid.")

THE BILL
YES
NO

THE BILL
NO

THE PRESIDENT

But the President's veto doesn't have to be the end of a bill. Congress can pass a bill over the President's veto if two-thirds of both the House and the Senate think the bill should be a law.

Chances are that two-thirds of the Senators and two-thirds of the Representatives would not like peanut butter and mayonnaise, and this bill would never get to be a law.

Why are laws about taxes and the army special?

Bills about taxes and money for armies are not like other bills. They can start only in the House of Representatives.

Since Representatives are elected every two years, they can lose their jobs pretty quickly. The delegates thought they would be closer to the people.

Why did the delegates invent the Supreme Court?

The delegates knew that there would need to be a court to decide fights between the states, and to decide if any of the states were passing laws that went against the Constitution. They had been using the British court

Article III establishes the Supreme Court.

system and expected their judges to go on following that tradition.

They knew that there would have to be a whole system of Federal Courts with a Supreme Court at the top, but they left out many details about how the courts would work.

The courts would be another check against any one group getting too much power. But how do you get an independent court?

The delegates decided to let the President nominate the Justices for the Supreme Court. However, the Senate would have to agree with the President's choice, or the President would have to suggest someone else.

How can we change the Constitution?

The delegates wanted their Constitution to last. They wanted people in the future to have a way to change the government without having another revolution.

They wanted their new Constitution to be easier to change than the old Articles of Confederation, which had said that nothing could be changed unless every single state agreed.

The Constitution spells out two ways it can be changed. One way would be to make major changes and to call another convention. It would take two-thirds of the states to call one.

This method has never been used.

The second way is to amend the Constitution.

Article V tells how the Constitution can be changed.

What is an amendment?

An amendment is a specific change in the Constitution. There have been amendments to end slavery and to give women the vote. All in all we have approved only twenty-six amendments.

It is not easy to change the Constitution with an amendment. An amendment has to be approved by two-thirds of both the Senate and the House of Representatives.

Then it is taken to the states, where it has to be voted on by either the state legislature or a special convention. Three-quarters of all the states must pass an amendment before it becomes part of the Constitution.

What was missing from the Constitution?

There was no Bill of Rights in the original Constitution. A Bill of Rights protects you, the individual, from the power of your government. The idea of a Bill of Rights, a list of things that the government cannot do, goes way back in English history, back to 1215, when the English lords made King John sign the Magna Carta.

Magna Carta *means "Great Charter." The charter listed rights that land owners and church leaders demanded from cruel King John.*

What are some of the rights in a Bill of Rights?

One of the rights guaranteed in a Bill of Rights is freedom of religion. Under English rule many colonists did not enjoy freedom to worship as they pleased. When James Madison was a young man in Virginia, the Church of England was the colony's official church. Baptists and Methodists were often thrown into jail.

After the Revolution, the state government of Virginia declared that all people should be free to worship as they choose. They made freedom of religion part of their Bill of Rights. The Virginia Bill of Rights also said that all men were free and equal. It forbade cruel and unusual punishment. It gave all people the right to trial by jury.

Many other states copied the Virginia Bill of Rights into their own Constitutions.

Why didn't the delegates put a Bill of Rights into the Constitution?

The issue of a bill of rights came up when the delegates were almost finished writing the Constitution. Everyone was tired.

George Mason was the author of the Virginia Bill of Rights. He was at the Philadelphia Convention, and he wanted the Constitution to have a Bill of Rights, too. He felt the most important job that the Constitution had to do was to make sure that government did not have too much power. Many delegates said it was enough that the thirteen states had Bills of Rights.

They voted not to put one in. Later they regretted it.

How did the Convention end?

By September, the delegates were ready to go home. They had been hard at work

for almost four months.

The delegates voted to give everything they had done to a committee to see if the writing was clear and understandable.

Gouverneur Morris was known as the best writer, so the committee gave the job to him. He wasn't supposed to change things, just check the spelling and grammar. But Morris was not above putting in a few of his own words. Just look what he did with the very first line. It had read: "We the people of the States of North Carolina, Virginia, Massachusetts, etc."

Morris changed it to "We, the people of the United States."

What a difference! Because Morris was right. If the Constitution was accepted, we would be a people, united — united by our new law.

What happened when the delegates signed the Constitution?

On September 17, the day they were all to sign the Constitution, Benjamin Franklin had written a speech. He tried to get up to give it, but he felt too weak. He asked his friend and fellow delegate from Philadelphia, James Wilson, to read it for him. Franklin said that there were many things in the Constitution he didn't agree with. But . . .

"Many a time in my life, I have been absolutely sure I was right, only to change my mind a year or two later. Some people never change their minds. They are always rather ridiculous. I once knew a dowager who told me her sister said to her, 'I don't know how it happens, Sister, but I meet

Thirty-nine delegates signed the Constitution.

with nobody but myself that is always in the right.' "

Luther Martin and many other delegates who didn't like the Constitution had already gone home. Only three delegates who were there refused to sign. George Mason refused to sign the Constitution because it had no Bill of Rights. Edmund Randolph of Virginia always had a hard time making up his mind, and he refused. He was worried he might be on the wrong side. Elbridge Gerry of Massachusetts also refused, but people called him a "Grumbletonian," someone who always grumbled.

One by one the other delegates, thirty-nine in all, came forward to sign the document. Each dipped the quill pen into the ink bottle and wrote his name carefully. Finally,

George Washington had to get up from his chair to write his name.

Benjamin Franklin looked at the empty chair. Franklin said painters always have a hard time showing the difference between a rising and a setting sun.

"I have often," said he, "looked at that (sun) behind the President without being able to tell whether it was rising or setting, but now . . . I have the happiness to know that is a rising and not a setting sun."

How did the thirteen states approve, or ratify, the new Constitution?

The Constitution had been written in secret. Now the delegates were going to find out what everyone else thought.

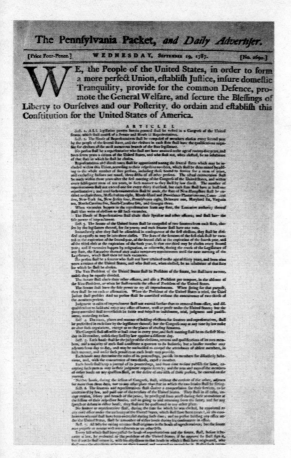

Two days after the delegates signed the Constitution, it was printed in newspapers like The Pennsylvania Packet and Daily Advertiser *for everyone to read.*

The delegates knew how hard it was to get all thirteen states to agree on anything. They said the Constitution had to be approved by just nine states in order to become the law of the land. They had come a long way. When they met in May, they were not even sure they should write a constitution. Now they not only had one, but they were saying it would go into effect even if all the states wouldn't agree.

Each state would have an election for delegates to a Convention to vote "yea" or "nay" on the Constitution.

Newspapers published the Constitution, and almost everyone had an opinion about it, good or bad. George Washington called it a "novel and astonishing spectacle of a whole people deliberating calmly on what form of government will be most conducive to their happiness."

Many people didn't like the Constitution because it had no Bill of Rights. "We promise to put one in," said some supporters of the Constitution, and that was indeed one of the first things the new government did. They are the first ten amendments to the Constitution, added in 1791.

Many people thought things were fine under the Articles of Confederation. But the people who wanted the Constitution had a big advantage over the people who didn't like it. The Constitution was exciting because it was new, and it was written down. All those who didn't like it could just grumble about what they didn't like.

When did we become "the United States?"

The fiercest battles for approval were fought in Virginia and New York. For a while it looked as if the Constitution would lose in these states, then, just before the Fourth of July 1788, the Constitutional Conventions in Virginia and New York voted "yea." New Hampshire had approved the Constitution a few days earlier, so now there were more than enough states for the nation to begin.

What a Fourth of July they celebrated that year! In New York City, ten white horses pulled a full-sized gun ship down the streets. They called the ship *The Alexander Hamilton*.

In Philadelphia, a ship renamed the *Rising Sun* boomed its cannons as five thousand paraders got ready to march. One of the floats, called *The Constitution*, was a carriage built in the shape of an eagle.

Why is the Constitution called a miracle?

George Washington called the Constitution a miracle. So did James Madison, and many historians have called it a miracle since then.

Is it a miracle because it was written so quickly? It took less than four months. But a bad Constitution could have been written just as fast.

Is it a miracle because it has lasted so long? Bad governments can last two hundred years.

In 1787, the United States had thirteen states and fewer than four million people. Today we have fifty states and more than 240 million people.

During the fight to ratify the Constitution, some people argued that if we were one nation, we would split up into special interests — the farmers would stick together, the merchants, Catholics against Protestants.

Madison wrote that joining together to lobby or pressure your government for your special interest is as important to liberty as air is to fire. Without it, liberty would die.

Madison thought that it was good if a republic was big. If the country was big enough, no one special interest could rule over the others. Madison and most of the other delegates wanted to make up a government that would never allow one group to have too much power over a smaller group.

Madison and Hamilton knew the nation would get bigger. The real miracle of the Constitution is that the men who wrote it had so much respect for the need of people to control and change their government. Otherwise, the piece of paper they were writing would never have lasted, except as a piece of paper under glass.

You can see the original Constitution in the National Archives Building in Washington, D.C.